METANOIA

The journey of spiritual conversion

Pratikhya Panda

ISBN 978-93-5610-117-3
© Pratikhya Panda 2022
Published in India 2022 by Pencil

A brand of

One Point Six Technologies Pvt. Ltd.
123, Building J2, Shram Seva Premises,
Wadala Truck Terminal, Wadala (E)
Mumbai 400037, Maharashtra, INDIA
E connect@thepencilapp.com
W www.thepencilapp.com

Author biography

Pratikhya Panda, the author, is a writer by passion.

She is from Bhubaneswar, India. At present, she is continuing as a student in DAV Public School. She is also an orator.

She has always taken a keen interest in literature. She started writing at a very young age, especially poems. According to her, framing the things that one experiences into words, is possible only when they learn from those experiences. Words are meant to be understood and so they need not be ornamented all the time.

She considers herself as a learner and so believes that her words are an expression of the lessons she's taught by life.

CONTENTS

Epigraph

"It's ordinary to love the beautiful.

but it's beautiful to love the ordinary.

Assume yourself being ordinary,

you'll start knowing the best person on the planet!"

-Pratikhya

Introduction

METANOIA

The conversion of a particular mindset is difficult, especially when it comes to people who have never experienced spirituality. Spirituality? What is spirituality defined by? It is not about believing a supreme power but knowing what the power is. The power could be anything, could be anyone.

Metanoia stands for 'spiritual conversion'. The journey that makes you witness true value of your own, discover yourself, is what spiritual conversion is.

The collection brings you the true essence of 'Metanoia'. Being a spiritual individual allows your thoughts to transcend. The chapters of METANOIA are the lessons to learn the definition of spirituality; the experiences, the morals, framed into one.

The set of writings will bring you the realisation of true love, pure affection, experience of individuality, transcendence, self-love and so much more, all in one!

Happy reading!

LIFE

Living and survival aren't the same thing, you know.

There are many reasons to live, and on reason for survival.

The one reason for survival is living,

Survival is so possible when you have those reasons to live. There are stages of life that one goes through along with undiscovered stories.

Spiritualism is thus defined to be achieved by souls who have known and discovered the reasons to live.

1. LIVE FOR THE REASONS

You know what? Live.

Live because there are so many places

that are waiting to be in

your box of memories you hide

under your pile of clothes.

Live because you are the one thing

that's missing from the sky

when the world talks about moon-less nights.

Live because your mother talks about you

and her eyes look like undiscovered

oysters with hazel pearls sitting

right inside them.

Live because your father remembers the day

you wrapped your entire hand around

his index finger, as if it happened

just the previous day.

Live because you were born to speak

the language of turning a house

into a home, and not of loitering at the edges

of unfamiliar graveyards.

Live because there are so many bizarre dreams

you still haven't seen and woke up

in the middle of the night to.

Live because there are so many cocoons

that haven't turned into butterflies just yet.

Live because there are so many new books

you haven't smelled yet, so many poems

you haven't written yet, so many stories

you haven't weaved yet.

Live because there are so many lives

you have saved till today, except your **OWN**.

THE COLOUR

Colours.

The beauty of colours is unbeatable.

The presence of colours makes something beautiful to us, makes us love that something. Imagine something colourless. Water? That slips off when you try holding it?

It's because of it's properties, philosophically it's nature.

The colour yellow, reminds you of the bright side. The prettiest of all, just because it defines light. Reminds you of something? Well, here's what I get from it.

2. DESCRIBE THE COLOUR YELLOW

Yellow reminds me of fireflies

packed in mason jars only to be set free;

reminding my heart how letting go might just be,

A beautiful thing after all.

Yellow is no less than the explosion

of confetti in the surprise party

Yellow is like the butterflies that reside

in the stomach of an orphan;

When he comes to know someone finally

plucked him from the field of sunflowers and

was going to take him home.

Home; yellow reminds me of home and all the confessions
and secrets

And "hey we survived another day of this pandemic"
dinners

That the enclosure of this home

holds — it reminds me of a three BHK painted in white

But my family?

They're the splashes of yellow for these boring walls.

Yellow makes me think about all the things

that I make it out of my bed, fold my sheets

with it's corners meeting at right angles

And treat myself with a cup of coffee —

Because I made it today, I made it out of my bed.

And yellow reminds me of all the days

I was nothing but kind to myself,

caressing the scars on my parched skin

And seeing the verses of my poems

blooming like hopeful, yellow sunflowers,

right there, right here.

LAUGHTER

Laughing always helps, it's a matter of escape after all.

A day without laughter is never a good day. Laughing not always means one being happy; sometimes, it helps you hide the emotions, the emotions you'd never show anyone except for your own self.

Laughing is sometimes a judgement. Sometimes judges out the fact of being actually happy and sometimes, being different from the other. But, it helps.

3.LAUGH A LITTLE TOO MUCH

The concept of reality is vague

And, forever a myth.

I laugh a little too much.

So they don't ask me, why I'm different.

Laughing always helps.

I look at the sky,

and see saturated sunshine.

My champagne, a bubbling contrast,

I believe many people, at once.

Mu canvas holds more colours than seven.

When you tell me your stories,

in my head, I'm painting them with my fingers,

along with you.

I laugh a little too much.

So I don't have to explain, why I'm different.

The moon looks bigger,

in this part of the world.

But it always reminds me of my small home.

I look at the trees passing by,

and think of the time passed by.

I ache and cry,

for no apparent reason.

But when they see me,

I laugh a little too much.

So they don't know, why I'm different.

THE PHASE

There's always a part of our life we want to be on loop.

That phase of life, that experience gives us grief, in a way that is beneficial.

A soul never altered by the threads binding people, will experience a part where they learn the truth; the truth of living, the truth of livelihood. Making a life of these truths, weaving it all together as they were all lies, is what will make you a success.

4.BRING BACK

Brittle memories of nonchalance,

from a time, once familiar.

How beautiful were those days!

Inquisitive eyes stooped at everything in daze.

Little hands armouring,

trembling feet.

The dropping tears braided,

into smiles so beautifully.

The innocence then, now,

embrace my soliloquy.

Innocence, bliss

oblivion, beautiful

memories, endless

that phase, golden days.

Cheerful smile ran through the street

memories dangling through sways,

those were the days, sweet.

To that time, I hail.

LITTLE THINGS

Little things. Little efforts.

Of course, efforts don't take much.

Attaining a state of happiness is what should be the motive.

People come and go. No one waits to see the happy side of us. Human is all together a plethora of experiences.

5.CALL ME IF YOU CAN

They come and go.

I write and forget.

They leave me with words,

so I don't regret.

You could be one of them,

I don't yet know.

Just a whiff of endorphin,

and into thin air, you'd go.

But you hold the car door open,

and tell me not to rush.

Little words and little things,

it really doesn't take much.

You lock my hands up

and my walls crumble down.

I scold myself to stop,

I never learnt how to own.

There's so much love inside me,

so much contempt.

I could gather them together,

only if I knew, you'd accept.

I started hopelessly hoping,

the day it began.

But if I run away,

call me if you can.

HELP

Stop!

You've done way too much.

You need some rest.

You need some help, maybe.

You need some happiness.

You need some appreciation.

You need some time.

You need some part of yourself...

6.HEAVENS!

Heavens!

Live a dream, it's late.

Heavens!

Show a path the dusk is near.

Heavens!

Have mercy, the bird needs rest.

Have mercy, the bird needs food.

Heavens!

Rain more sunrays.

And sprinkle, more fragrances.

Heavens!

Heavens!

FIGHT

Spiritualism has its roots from fighting, fighting with your own shadow.

The shadow is what you actually are, unfiltered.

The shadow is the real side of you.

The shadow never changes.

The shadow is away of all the morals you're taught.

The shadow is a framework of the lessons you've built in.

The shadow is the true definition of no one but you.

7.THE BATTLE

After my battle with the world,

I realise that how naive was I,

wanting to grow up faster,

because time gave me experience

and stole my innocence.

If only we could see the world through,

their innocent and truthful eyes,

and perceive the radiance,

in their contagious smiles.

I swear, these bubbly hearts could

teach us the way of living life.

These innocent hearts don't know,

what's coming up next.

Who loves them the most now,

will hurt them the next.

They'll someday find find out,

what growing up means.

And then they'll wish,

they could just rewind,

every single one,

of those little things.

THE WEAPON

Smile.

I define it as a weapon. Thinking of a person who you see smiling every single day confuses you.

Is that person really happy?

Is that person hiding something behind that evil smile?

Is that person trying hard to share something?

Is that person expecting something in return for that smile?

You never know.

8.THE SMILE

People catch her smiling,

when she's feeling low, or,

life is turning her blue.

She explains her sadness,

carrying pain in her smile.

But everytime,

she wears her smile.

Everything which hurts her,

she smiles and pretends,

it doesn't.

Her smiles hide her scars,

and reflects her strength.

It's the crown,

she always wears,

and will never let it fall!

EFFORTS

All it takes is some efforts, some memories you make with them.

There are not many things one could worry about.

There are not few things that can make one satisfied.

Being careful was never a habit, it is adapted.

Being nonchalant could've been a habit, if adapted.

The memory lane, you pass through it.

The album of those photographs you've clicked in your mind, are the best shots.

No edits and always unfiltered.

9.EFFORTS TO REALISE

I can hear water trickling down the roof,

like an old soul's careful footsteps.

Slowly walking through darkness,

touching the wall at every step.

Raindrops are talking continuously outside,

from whispers to screams, soft talks.

Maybe gossips, long at times,

lost at times, or maybe, to the winds.

My efforts to decipher them are foolish,

though my mind, spreads it's wings.

Thinking of various things,

the raindrops could worry about.

Just yesterday, it was dusty,

and the smokes and flakes added.

Seeping down would have been difficult,

let out a thunder, out of frustration.

The efforts to keep us green are tiring,

trying to reach every corner, every leaf.

Every venture drains her light,

heavier her plight, darker the rains.

THE DIFFERENCE

Growing up.

It was never that easy as it did sound.

I still remember two raindrops running down the window pane and silly me assuming, it was a race.

I still remember when I got my first amount of money as my own income; of course, it was not too much, just a note of five hundred.

The happiness, never did cost me. Growing up, included holding onto things, have a perspective different than my own.

10.GROWING UP

A part of growing up,

also includes fading interests,

in things you used to be so excited about.

A part of growing up,

includes understanding things from,

someone else's perspectives,

even before you've been told to.

A part of growing up,

tells us to hold onto things,

for too long that are worth it,

and a part of it tells us to let go

of situations that do not hold power over us.

A part of growing up is smiling,

and sharing secrets within.

And most importantly, a part of growing up,

holds on to the wrong wish,

we made to grow up so fast.

KARMA

Look at your beautiful hands.

The work they did, the number of handshakes they've approached to.

I've always been a believer of karma, always been told about the role of these hands.

There's so much to learn from them.

They've been a medium of being congratulated, they've been a part of the last goodbye.

Over all, they allow the voice for what you do.

11.THE DEEDS

I look at my hands and think,

how beautiful it is that these hands,

have cupped my eyes during

a game of peekaboo,

with a stranger's baby on the bus,

And these hands have also trembled,

during goodbyes that were either long,

overdue, or too soon.

It is such a soft thought,

that my hands have held rusty mics,

while telling the world about,

my broken stories,

and death and bodies, that have died five days of the week
and still,

come back to life for more.

these are the same hands

that have brushed against theirs,

during random passing, of a coffee mug.

These are the same hands that have

held the tighter grip, during every single goodbye.

These are the same hands, that have picked up the pen,

instead of the knife on nights,

when it gets too cold,

and too dark, and too claustrophobic.

I look at my hands and think,

how these hands have held,

dying dreams and blooming flowers,

how these hands have known,

too tender or too destructive —

and nothing in between.

REAL

"The concept of reality is vague, and forever a myth."

Real.

Being real is what makes one appreciable. Reality does cost way too much, but pays back way more than it costs.

Reality brings in acceptance, the power of accepting reality of all around us.

12.REALITY

I'm real,

as real can be,

not just a fragment of imagination,

that they thought can never come to be.

I'm real, when I give you warmth,

even when I'm freezing,

from the cold of loneliness.

I'm real, when I smile,

although, I may be breaking within,

into million irrevocable pieces.

I'm real, when all I want is their joy,

even if it means,

I've to part with my own, never to own it again.

I'm real, when all I know is to give,

and they take, forever and ever,

greedily digging, into an empty pit.

I'm real, when I love unconditionally

and yet get trampled,walked over,

used and brushed aside selfishly.

I'm very real, when you painted shades,

as thought, right,erasing what I was,

to an extent that I didn't know myself.

Yes I am real,

broken, yet spirited.

I am, **A FRAGILE REALITY.**